Macdonald Careers

Airport

Arthur Reed

Macdonald Educational

Series Editor Philippa Stewart
Editor Caroline Russum
Design Peter Benoist
Production Philip Hughes
Picture Research Jenny Golden

Macdonald Educational Ltd
Holywell House
Worship Street
London EC2A 2EN

First published 1978
© Macdonald Educational Ltd

ISBN 0 382 06196 9

Published in the United
States by Silver Burdett
Company, Morristown, N.J.
1978 Printing

Library of Congress
Catalog Card No. 78-61230

Airport

Contents

A modern airport

In 1977 there were many thousands of flights in all parts of the world, carrying a total of over 620 million passengers. In years to come the number of flights will rise steadily. To cater for the ever-increasing numbers of passengers, bigger and better airports are constantly being built.

These airports must be fitted out with the most up-to-date aids to safety. Long, wide runways; radar equipment enabling air traffic controllers to 'see' the planes when they are miles away; blind-landing systems

Charles de Gaulle Airport, 16 kilometres to the north of Paris, is one of Europe's most modern. Opened in the early 1970s, it was designed for the future, with plenty of space to build more terminal buildings. The first terminal is circular with a series of 'satellites' from which people board their planes, and which they reach underground on moving walkways. Car parking is on the terminal's upper floors. Only one house had to be demolished when Charles de Gaulle Airport was built, but it took kilometres of fertile farmland.

◀ Most modern airports are difficult to reach from the cities which they serve, but Charles de Gaulle Airport has a train which runs right into the airport from the heart of Paris. London's Heathrow Airport now has the same facility, but the line was only opened in 1977, 31 years after the airport began operations. At Charles de Gaulle, the railway line was designed in right from the start. In the future no new airport will be built anywhere in the world without a quick and efficient system of transport, able to move millions of people a year, built into its basic design.

for use in thick fog: these are just some of the technological advances by which flying is being made safer.

Airport planners must provide enormous terminal buildings to cater for arriving and departing passengers. These terminals must be fitted with facilities such as shops, banks and restaurants. To get the passengers speedily to and from the terminals, there must be networks of roads and railways, as well as huge car parks where people can leave their cars while they are away on business or holiday.

A modern airport is just like a small city. It has an army of workers doing hundreds of different jobs to keep it going day and night, all through the year. Charles de Gaulle Airport, illustrated on this page, has a staff of 17,000 to cope with the 7.7 million passengers who pass through each year.

Many airport jobs are very specialized, requiring years of training. Others are less skilled. This book describes how airports operate and some of the many jobs to be found in these exciting and busy workplaces.

▶ Charles de Gaulle Airport has some of the latest models of expanding bridges through which passengers walk to board the planes. The system speeds up departures and arrivals, keeps the travellers dry and does away with steps.

◀ These space-age tubes inside the circular terminal at Charles de Gaulle Airport take passengers on moving walkways between the various airport levels. Arriving and departing passengers are directed to different floors so that the traffic flows do not meet. Sign-posting is clear and in many languages so that although Charles de Gaulle is a big and confusing place, it is difficult to get lost.

▶ In the baggage arrivals hall, passengers pick up their luggage from a series of endless belts.

The passenger terminal

From the moment a passenger books a flight to the moment he finally boards the plane, a great deal of work is done behind the scenes to ensure that all goes smoothly. Just making certain that the right number of passengers board the right plane takes a lot of careful planning by the airlines.

All of the big airlines today have computers into which details of the passengers and their flights are fed when they book their tickets. When a passenger checks in at the airport, the check-in clerk taps out the number of his ticket on a sort of typewriter keyboard. A television set, linked to the central computer, prints out information which tells the clerk if the ticket held by the passenger is correct. Televisions in the airline's offices world-wide are linked into the computer. In the case of Air France, a clerk in New York can 'ask' the computer in Paris about a particular ticket and receive an answer in seconds.

While the passengers wait for their flight, other people are busy at work making sure that the luggage they have just checked in is sorted and en route for the right plane. At the same time, the load control department is working out how much fuel their plane will need for its trip, taking into account the total number of passengers and the weight of their luggage. And yet other airline workers are collecting information on their flight, so that departure boards and flight announcements are kept up-to-date.

▲ Passengers may arrive at an airport in a variety of ways—by car, by taxi, by train or by bus. Here a bus pulls up outside one of the modern airline terminals at John F Kennedy, the main international airport of New York. The passengers then take their luggage to the check-in counter.

▼ At the check-in desks, the passengers present their tickets to the clerks who check the booking with the airline computer. They next weigh the luggage, label it for its destination, and send it off on a conveyor belt for loading. They then issue the passenger with a card for boarding the plane.

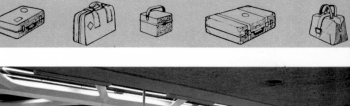

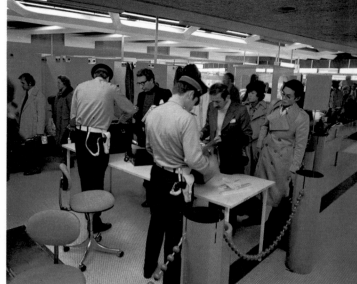

▼ While they are waiting for their flight to be called, passengers sit in a lounge where they can have a drink and a meal. An electronic board gives flight details and warns of delays.

▼ The flight is called and the passengers walk out to the airliner. Sometimes they are taken out by bus, or board through an enclosed pier which links with the plane door.

◄ Before boarding, every passenger must pass through a security check.

▼ All modern airports have banks and shops for last-minute purchases.

► Out on the apron, the luggage is being loaded on to the plane. The loaders are using a mechanical belt which takes the cases right into the plane's hold.

7

Passenger handling staff

▲ Airline sales staff need to know their way around complicated time-tables and lists of fares.

Being a steward or stewardess is a glamorous job in the eyes of the public, but there are plenty of workers on the ground at airports who deal with passengers, and who play just as important a part as those who fly. Passenger handling staff can be employed either by the authority which runs the airport, the airlines, or by tour and travel operators. Most of them wear uniform. Their task is to smooth the path of passengers or visitors to airports who may be bewildered, and even just a little bit frightened, in a strange, noisy and confusing world.

Passenger service assistants

These men and women come into contact with the public both face-to-face and on the telephone. Their work includes reserving seats, issuing air tickets, checking passengers in for their flights, escorting, advising, assisting and controlling passengers and their baggage, allocating seats on the planes and escorting the passengers to the door of the aircraft.

As they are sometimes dealing with people who are under a certain amount of stress, passenger service assistants need good poise and the ability to work coolly under pressure. They must be adaptable so that they can deal with a rapidly changing situation without getting flustered. Above all they must get on well with a wide variety of people. Families with young children and babies, children travelling on their own, elderly or sick passengers, VIPs (Very Important Passengers) such as royalty, all have to be treated in the same friendly, patient and tactful manner.

The public judge the airport or the airline for which they work by them, so passenger service assistants must be well groomed. A knowledge of some foreign language is a help, as they will meet passengers of many different nationalities. They must also be prepared to work unusual hours.

Passenger service assistants are often employed at first for a six-month pro-bationary period, during which a watch is kept on their standard of work. If it is satisfactory, they are likely to be offered a post on the permanent staff.

There are also opportunities for work in the summer when most airlines have to engage extra temporary staff to cope with the rush of holiday and tourist passengers. Such a period of short service can often give the worker a chance to decide whether he or she would really like being on the permanent staff.

The assistants are expected to use a certain amount of technical equipment such as computer-controlled reservations systems, public address systems and portable radio transmitters. This equipment is, however, fairly simple to operate after a short spell of training, which is given by the employer.

Sales staff

Selling air tickets to the public is a specialized job. The men and women who do it must have detailed knowledge of the routes and services of their own airline and most of the others in the world, and also of the very complicated lists of fares.

The large majority of these workers will be employed either in the central ticket office at their airline's headquarters, where they talk to the public or travel agents wishing to buy tickets over the telephone, or in high street airline offices, where they sell tickets both by phone or over the counter.

But there are also ticket desks at airports where passengers can buy tickets for flights that day or have their tickets changed to different flights or routes.

► Working in the airport nursery is a rewarding job for those who enjoy children.

◄ Every airport has an information desk where passengers' queries are dealt with quickly and efficiently.

▼ At most airports porters are on hand to help passengers with their heavy luggage.

Porter

Luggage porters have an important role in keeping passengers moving through airports. Many airport authorities now provide luggage trolleys on which you can push your own luggage, but those with lots of bags, or the elderly and infirm still prefer to have their luggage taken care of.

At most airports porters have a uniform provided by the airport authority. They meet the taxis and cars bringing passengers to the airport and carry their luggage to the check-in desk of the airline with which they are flying.

They also meet people coming off incoming flights, carrying their bags through Customs control and out to whatever form of transport is to take them from the airport. They are among the first people with whom foreigners have any contact and so are often asked for information about the airport and the country as a whole.

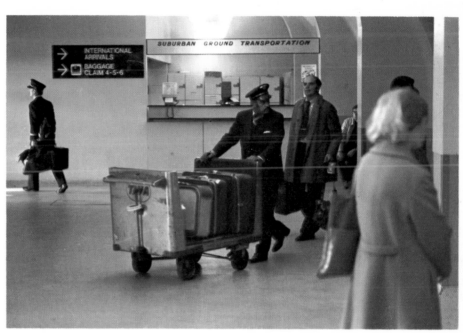

Travel representative or courier

When large parties of people are travelling together on a charter flight, the tour company which has arranged the travel often has a uniformed representative present at the airport before departure to make sure that everybody is checked in, that their luggage is labelled, and that they get to the plane on time.

Airport information representative

Most of the big airports throughout the world now have their own staff of representatives, usually girls wearing a distinctive uniform, who work behind an information desk, or move among the public on the airport concourses answering questions. They have to cope with a wide variety of queries, from where the nearest telephone boxes are situated, to how to find a lost child. Airport information representatives must remain calm and patient at all times. They will usually speak one or more foreign languages.

Children's nurse

Most big airports have a children's nursery or crèche where parents can leave their children for a short time while they go off to have a meal before their flight. One of the parents is usually expected to return every 20 minutes to see if the children are happy.

The nurseries are equipped with toys and games and are bright, cheerful places so that the boys and girls left in them feel at home. They are staffed by women who have been trained as children's nurses. Once again, like all the people mentioned in this section, the nurses must expect to work unusual hours, often in the evening and at weekends.

◄ A passenger service assistant with her young charges. She is responsible for looking after them until they board their plane.

Inside the plane

On the plane the passengers take their seats. Usually the seats are numbered and the cabin crew have to make sure that everyone is sitting in the right place. On most flights today passengers can choose in advance whether they want to sit in a smoking or non-smoking area.

Before take-off the 'no-smoking' and 'fasten seat belts' signs are lit up in the cabin. These are switched off once the plane is in the air but the stewards and stewardesses often advise passengers to keep their seat belts fastened loosely during the flight in case the plane is bumped about by turbulent air.

There are up to 20 members of cabin staff on board a jumbo jet to look after 350 passengers. Before boarding, the staff are briefed by the chief steward or purser on any special problems. On a typical flight they may have to cope with an invalid passenger who needs a wheel-chair, a young boy or girl who needs looking after because he or she is travelling alone, and someone who has asked for a special meal for religious or dietary reasons.

Before take-off a member of the cabin crew shows the passengers where the emergency exits are in case they have to leave the plane in a hurry after a crash. He or she also demonstrates the emergency oxygen system. Because airliners fly high where there is not much air to breathe, air has to be pumped into the planes. If the supply fails, oxygen masks linked to separate bottles of air fall down automatically from the roof racks so that the passengers can breathe.

As soon as the plane has taken off, the cabin staff change into overalls and start serving drinks, food and duty-free goods. They work hard in very cramped surroundings. On a short flight of an hour and a half the stewards and stewardesses can spend a total of only $3\frac{1}{2}$ minutes attending to each passenger.

Meals, which are prepared in the airline's own kitchens, are placed in the aircraft's galleys before the flight. Just before serving the meals are put into a micro-wave oven which heats them up in 30 seconds.

At the end of the meal, the cabin staff have many other jobs to do, such as clearing away the trays, handing out hot towels to the passengers, distributing pillows and blankets if the flight is at night, serving tea and coffee and other drinks on request, and generally making sure that the travellers are comfortable.

When the flight is over and the passengers have left the plane, the cabin crew still have a number of duties to do. They make sure the galleys are left tidy and check the bar and account for the sales they have made, often in many different currencies.

▲ Welcome aboard; a stewardess uses the public address system to talk to the passengers during a flight. She tells them how long it will take, and at what height and speed the plane will be flying.

Boeing 747 B Jumbo

capacity up to 500 passengers

engine with 45,000 lb thrust

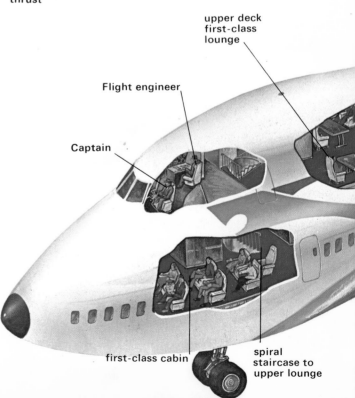

upper deck first-class lounge

Flight engineer

Captain

first-class cabin

spiral staircase to upper lounge

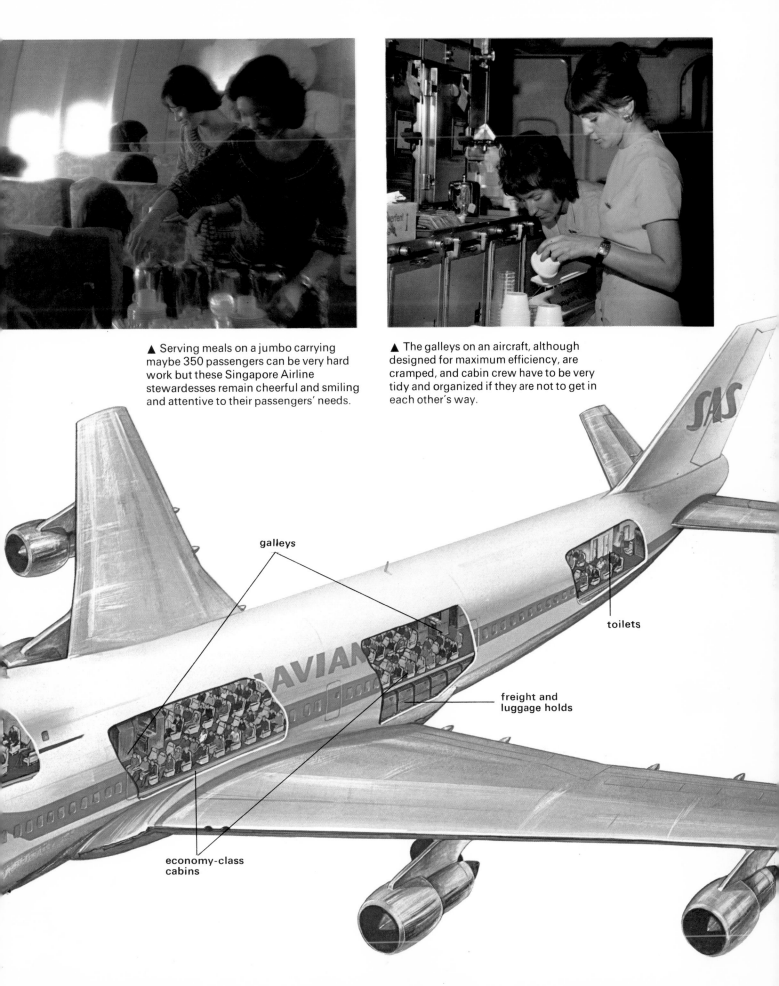

▲ Serving meals on a jumbo carrying maybe 350 passengers can be very hard work but these Singapore Airline stewardesses remain cheerful and smiling and attentive to their passengers' needs.

▲ The galleys on an aircraft, although designed for maximum efficiency, are cramped, and cabin crew have to be very tidy and organized if they are not to get in each other's way.

galleys

toilets

freight and luggage holds

economy-class cabins

Take-off and cruise

Before a flight, the flight crew, usually two pilots and, on a long flight, a flight engineer, report to the flight operations centre for briefing. Here they are told what weather to expect on the way, what route they should take, and what height they should fly. They work out how much fuel they will need, including a reserve amount in case the airport for which they are heading is foggy and they have to fly on somewhere else. Pre-flight planning can often take an hour or more.

1 Well before the flight is due to leave, pilots board the airliner to go through a long list of checks to see that everything works properly.

2 The flight engineer too has a list of checks to make.

3 In the cabin passengers are welcomed by stewardesses and stewards and shown where to sit. Cabin staff then close the doors of the airliner, and take their own seats.

4 The captain talks to the control tower by radio and is given permission to start engines and to begin to taxi towards the runway.

5 Seen through the cockpit window, a flight despatcher makes a last check of the airliner and then gives the crew the 'thumbs up' as clearance to move off.

6 Controllers watch the plane as it taxis towards the runway, making sure it keeps clear of other aircraft and vehicles on the ground.

7 The controllers are aided at modern airports by radar (inset) which gives a picture of the whole airport. The plane reaches the runway, and lines up for take-off.

With permission to taxi given by the control tower, a tractor tug pushes the airliner away from the pier. The tow bar is then uncoupled and the tractor moves away.

Although they are talking to the tower by radio, the only physical contact which the pilots have with the ground at this stage is with a despatcher over a line plugged into the plane. He makes sure the way is clear for taxiing.

The despatcher then disconnects his line and the plane moves off to the runway. Sometimes it may have to queue behind a dozen more planes before its turn to take off comes. Then, at last, the tower says that take-off can begin.

Take-off (illustrated below) and landing are the most demanding parts of a pilot's job. On most flights the pilot will switch in to the automatic pilot once the plane is on course. This is an electronic device which flies the plane from one radio station on the ground to another, without the crew having to touch the controls.

On short flights, such as that between London and Paris, which can take as little as 40 minutes between take-off and touch-down, the pilots are busy all the time. No sooner has the plane climbed to its cruising height where it begins to fly level, than it has to start to descend again. But on long-distance flights such as that between New York and Tokyo, taking 12 hours or more, the pilots have long periods when they do not actually have to fly the plane.

On these long hauls one of the pilots at least must be watching the instruments at all times. They take it in turns to eat their meals, even eating different food, so that if something is bad, they will not both suffer from food poisoning.

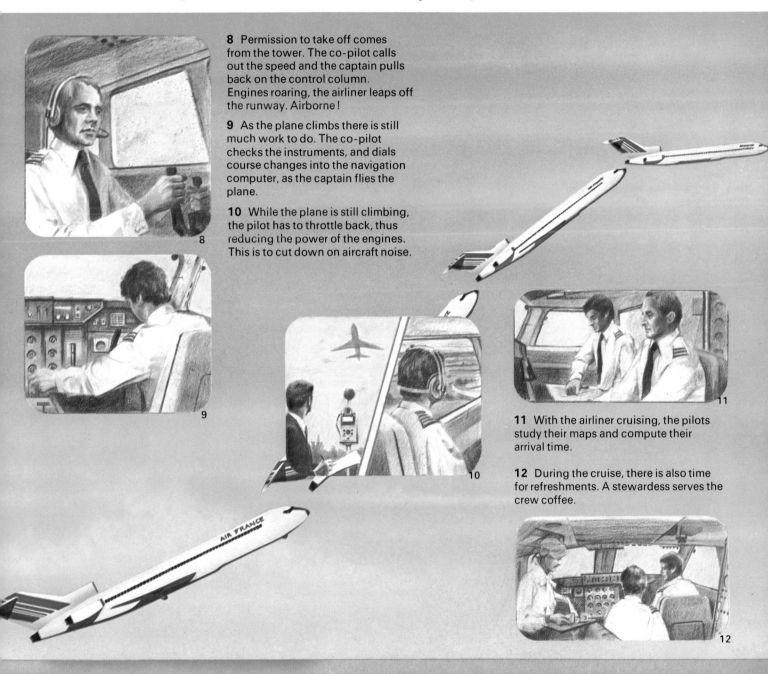

8 Permission to take off comes from the tower. The co-pilot calls out the speed and the captain pulls back on the control column. Engines roaring, the airliner leaps off the runway. Airborne!

9 As the plane climbs there is still much work to do. The co-pilot checks the instruments, and dials course changes into the navigation computer, as the captain flies the plane.

10 While the plane is still climbing, the pilot has to throttle back, thus reducing the power of the engines. This is to cut down on aircraft noise.

11 With the airliner cruising, the pilots study their maps and compute their arrival time.

12 During the cruise, there is also time for refreshments. A stewardess serves the crew coffee.

Depending on its type and how heavily it is loaded, every plane takes a different distance to take off. A three-engined jet with 100 passengers would be lifting its nose after 42 seconds. Take-off would come two seconds later.

By this time the plane has travelled about 2½ kilometres. 54 seconds after take-off run has begun the plane is 30 metres above the ground and climbing hard with engines at full thrust. At 460 metres the pilots throttle back.

This is to comply with the noise abatement rules. Microphones are installed on the ground under the take-off path to make sure that planes do not make too much noise and annoy people who live nearby.

The flight crew

The crew of an airliner consists of the pilots on the flight deck—assisted by a flight engineer on the larger airliners—and the stewards and stewardesses looking after the passengers in the cabin. Each crew member has a part to play in the safe and successful conclusion of every flight, but the captain, sitting in the left-hand seat on the flight deck, is in overall charge of the plane, its crew, its passengers and all its other contents. When one considers that there may be as many as 400 passengers on board, that the plane itself could cost £10m to buy, and its cargo could be worth millions of pounds as well, it can be seen that it is a very responsible task.

Pilot

Flying a plane of any size, whether it is a single-seater or a Concorde whisking 100 passengers across oceans at 2,000 kph needs a high level of skill, alertness, intelligence, and a great deal of dedication.

As with most jobs connected with airports, pilots must be ready to work at all hours of the day and night. They will certainly not go into the business if what they want is a 'nine-to-five' existence.

On the other hand, governments lay down very strict rules on just how long each day or week pilots can work. Obviously, if a pilot became too tired, his concentration could be affected and accidents could happen. In Britain, pilots are not allowed to be on duty for more than 50 hours each week, and cannot fly for more than 14 hours at a time.

Pilots used to be recruited largely from the forces. This source is now drying up in many countries, and special training schools have been opened. Some are run by the airlines, others are privately-owned. Most students join such courses straight from school or after university training.

▲ Russian airlines have been using women pilots for years. Today other airlines are following their example.

Airlines sponsor young men, and in a few cases young women, who they think will make good pilots, sending them to their own training schools, or paying for them to take courses at commercial flying schools, often abroad.

Candidates for pilot training are usually expected to be good at science subjects. Physical fitness, including excellent vision without glasses, is vital, and there are repeated medical checks throughout the pilot's career. Pilots normally retire at the age of 55 or 60, depending on the airline.

Training courses take around 20 months, during which students study a wide range of scientific and technical subjects, from aircraft design to aviation law. At an early stage in the course they will start to learn to fly in light aircraft with an instructor. Soon they will go solo, and by the end of the course they will probably have spent over 200 hours in the air.

The young pilot will then be posted to an airline as a junior officer. Here he will continue to study, flying on the flight deck of the big jets and watching and learning all the time until the day comes when he is assessed as proficient enough to take his place in the pilot team.

As the years pass he will learn to fly bigger and bigger planes and probably work his way up to captain. His skills will be constantly tested and checked throughout his career.

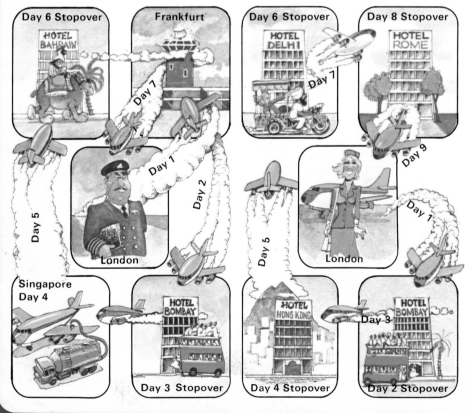

◄ Join an airline and see the world? These examples of a typical week for a pilot and a stewardess may seem exciting, but one hotel looks very much like another!

▲ Student pilots must learn to fly light aircraft before they can take the controls of large aircraft.

Flight engineer

Flight engineers are generally not pilots, but usually have a background in aviation engineering on the ground. Their job is to be responsible to the captain for the way in which the plane's electrical, fuel and mechanical systems perform. A flight engineer will be able to tell what has caused any faults in the systems, and will report these to the ground engineers when the flight is over.

During the flight he will keep a constant watch on the way the engines are running, making tiny adjustments to the throttle levers so that they use fuel as economically as possible. He takes part in the checks which the pilots have to make before, during and after a flight. He is a very important member of the flight-deck crew, taking much of the work load off the shoulders of the pilots, and leaving them free to concentrate on the actual flying of the plane.

Some flight engineers take flying courses and become pilots. Others eventually graduate to important administration jobs in aircraft engineering on the ground.

Cabin staff

Like pilots and flight engineers, stewards and stewardesses are expected to work unusual hours and will often be away from home for long periods. In its own way their job is just as demanding as that of the flight crew. Cabin staff meet the travelling public at very close quarters, and the airline whose uniform they wear is often judged by the way they perform.

They must, therefore, be polite, cheerful, patient, efficient and unflustered in the most difficult circumstances. Air travellers are often tired, bewildered and even frightened. Under these stresses they can become very demanding, sometimes even rude. Cabin staff must also be prepared to look after the elderly, the ill, and the very young, and to serve and clear away meals in the confined space of an airliner cabin.

They are, in fact, a mixture of receptionist, clerk, nurse, waitress, barmaid, companion, nanny, guide and adviser. At the same time, they have an important part to play in the safe and efficient operation of the flight. They make sure the doors are properly closed before take-off, and demonstrate the safety equipment and emergency oxygen masks. They are trained to keep their heads in an emergency and help their passengers to evacuate the plane in the shortest possible time.

Women are generally recruited as cabin staff between the ages of 20 and 27, men between the ages of 20 and 30. Airlines look for people with good health, good appearance and posture, and an easy, confident manner. A sound general education is required, and proficiency in languages is an obvious asset.

A drawback is that the career can be relatively short, particularly for women, for some airlines retire stewardesses after ten years of service. This rule is gradually being relaxed, and there are other airlines today with young grandmothers among their cabin crew.

Training for cabin crew lasts around five to six weeks in the airline school. Much of the time is spent working inside a full-scale model of an airliner built inside the classroom. The students learn about catering, Customs, immigration, foreign money exchange, safety and first-aid. At least one big airline insists that their cabin staff can swim.

In charge of every cabin crew there is a chief steward or stewardess who is promoted to the post on both length of service and ability. They have to undergo further training before taking up this responsible post.

▼ Cabin staff must be confident of handling even the tiniest baby.

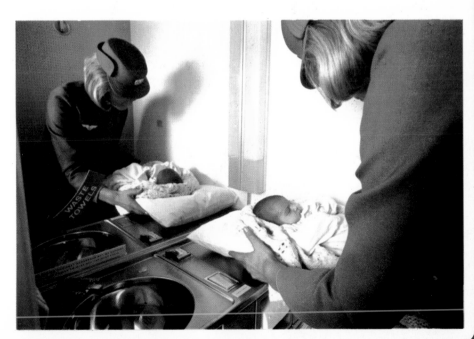

Controlling the planes

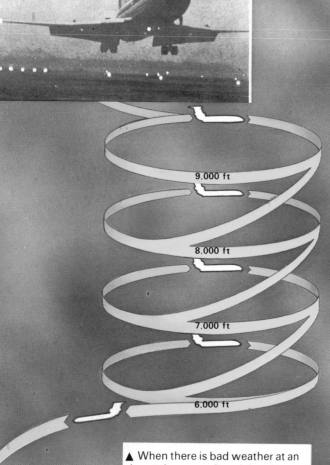

All flights depend for their safe departure and arrival on hundreds of men and women on the ground who monitor their progress throughout and instruct their pilots on take-off and landing.

While a plane is on the ground, its movements are directed by a ground controller in the glass room at the top of the control tower.

A few airports have ground-control radar. This enables controllers to see everything which is moving on the airport, even in the foggiest weather. Radar is a device whereby a revolving aerial sends out radio waves in all directions. These waves bounce back off solid objects such as aircraft and cars, which then show up as little blobs on television screens in the control tower.

After the airliner has taken off, the airport controller hands over to area controllers. These people work in a building away from the airport. On their strong radar sets they can see almost every plane that is flying in an area as big as Britain—up to 300 planes at a time on busy days.

The controllers can identify each plane because every blob on their screens has a code number behind it. From this they can tell which airline each plane belongs to and where it is going. If they see two blobs moving dangerously close to one another, the controllers can radio to the pilots of the planes which they represent and warn them to move apart. They must think quickly in such cases. When two planes are cruising, they could be approaching one another at a total speed of over 1,600 kph and the pilots would have no more than 30 seconds to take avoiding action.

Approach controllers are the men who help the plane to land. On their radar screens they can see if an airliner is too high or too low as it puts its nose down towards the airport runway, and can instruct the pilot by radio accordingly.

9,000 ft

8,000 ft

7,000 ft

6,000 ft

▲ When there is bad weather at an airport there are often delays in landing so that planes have to queue up. While they are waiting their turn to land they are 'stacked' by the controllers, flying round and round a radio beacon at 1,000-feet (300-metre) intervals, gradually moving down the stack until it is their turn to approach the runway.

▶ Planes can land automatically even though the pilots cannot see very far ahead. An electronic black box in the plane links up with a radio beam from the runway and flies the airliner down without the pilots having to place their hands on the controls.

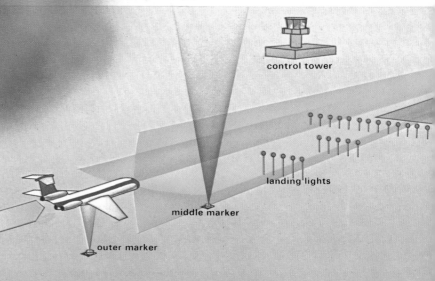

control tower

landing lights

middle marker

outer marker

▲ Air traffic controllers controlling take-offs at Düsseldorf Airport, Germany.

► A greatly simplified version of the maps pilots carry in the cockpit to help them find their way from one airport to another. It shows the upper airways, radio beacons, airports and military flight areas in southern Germany. To make sure planes flying the same airways are kept apart, those at 8,000, 10,000, 12,000 or 14,000 feet go one way, and those at odd-number heights in the opposite direction.

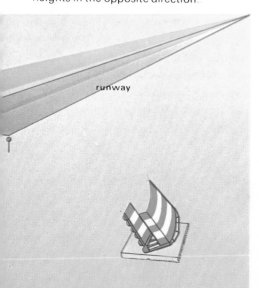

runway

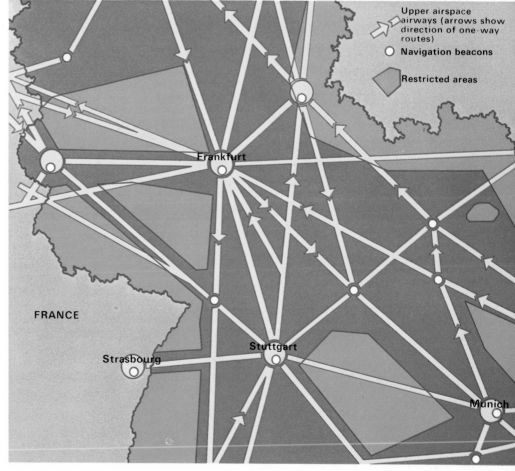

Upper airspace airways (arrows show direction of one-way routes)

◯ Navigation beacons

Restricted areas

Frankfurt

FRANCE

Strasbourg

Stuttgart

Munich

Air Traffic Controllers

Although they work on the ground, air traffic controllers have the lives of thousands of passengers in their hands each day. They watch the progress of the planes on their radar screens and talk to the pilots over the radio, telling them which direction to take, and making sure that planes do not fly too dangerously close to each other. The work requires a high level of concentration, but it also has a high level of job satisfaction.

Training

Air traffic control in many countries is based on the British system, and many foreign students are sent to Britain for training by either the Civil Aviation Authorities or private companies.

The CAA has a four-week course for young people who have no previous knowledge of aviation. It explains the duties of the air traffic controller and gives them a grounding in such subjects as air law, navigation and weather study. They then go to a flying school and learn to fly to private pilot licence standard.

Then follows a ten-week course for cadets, and also for adult students with some knowledge of general aviation. They learn more about air traffic services, air law, radio procedures and aircraft recognition. After that comes a succession of further courses during which the students learn the mysteries of radar, and work in control towers at airports controlling airliners on exercises.

The CAA also runs a technical staff course during which air traffic controllers learn about accident investigation, the control of supersonic airliners and the safety services. Air traffic controllers are encouraged to take flights on the flight decks of airliners on regular flights so that they can learn the pilot's view of their job.

Computer courses are also available for controllers. Computers are being used more and more as an aid to air traffic control. In future they will be used to tell controllers how far planes should fly apart, and warn them when two airliners get too close.

Air traffic controllers in all parts of the world must expect to learn English, as this is the official international language of aviation. All conversations between the ground and planes should be in English to avoid any possibility of misunderstandings. The international phonetic alphabet shown on the opposite page is also used to make the identification of flights as clear as possible. Failure to use English has caused at least one bad mid-air collision in which nearly 200 people were killed.

Obviously, air traffic controllers must be highly responsible people, level-headed in a crisis, with the ability to make quick, correct decisions. A high standard of physical fitness is essential, with excellent eyesight, as much of the time on duty is spent concentrating on the radar screen.

Airspace

When fully trained, controllers will be assigned to one of a number of different areas of airspace. These areas are carefully set out, and include the following:—

Controlled airspace. This covers the area around the main airports, and the main traffic lanes from them. In these areas all planes are under the firm control of air traffic control, and must have the correct equipment to enable them to navigate and talk to the ground.

Upper airspace. Under British rules, this covers the area between 24,500 feet (7,470 metres) and 46,000 feet (13,750 metres).

Middle airspace. This is between 8,000 feet (2,400 metres) and 24,500 feet (7,470 metres). Planes can fly either by using their instruments in the cockpit, or by visual flying rules—that is, by the pilot looking out of the window. A controller working the middle airspace would 'hand over' a climbing plane to his upper airspace colleague as it was about to pass through 24,500 feet.

Control centres

Many controllers find jobs at one of the main air traffic control centres. In Britain there are three: one at West Drayton, just outside Heathrow airport, London; one at Preston, in the north of England, and one at Prestwick, in Scotland. These centres control planes in the upper and sometimes middle airspace as they fly down the main airways corridors. The British centres mentioned above deal with over one million planes every year.

The heart of these centres are the big control rooms where controllers and their assistants group round the radar displays. In the past, controllers had to work in darkened rooms in order to see their screens clearly. But the latest sets are so bright that they can be viewed in clear daylight. Even so, the work of controlling three or four planes at once requires such a high degree of concentration that the controllers are relieved every hour so that they can have a rest before returning to their job.

In addition to the radar displays, the controllers have a wide range of technical devices to help them. They are given reports on every flight passing through their control, constantly brought up to date by their assistants. They can speak directly over the radio with the flight crews of the planes they are controlling, and also with other controllers in other parts of the country. And closed-circuit television screens display up-to-the-minute information on weather and conditions at airports.

◄ A general view inside a big air traffic control centre. The controllers watch the progress of hundreds of airliners on their radar screens and are presented with information on all flights by a special computer.

▼ A close-up of a controller at one of the radar screens. The controller can tell from the 'blips' on it just what each airliner is doing, and she can talk to the pilots by radio, warning them if their aircraft is moving too close to another for safety. In her hand are flight strips, giving details of each flight under her control.

▲ A mobile ground controller keeps in touch by radio with the control tower. His job is to see that all taxiways are kept clear so that the airliners can move around safely.

Aerodrome services or ground controllers

Air traffic controllers based in the control tower situated on the airport itself help planes to approach the airport, land and take off. They are also responsible for the safe movement of aircraft and vehicles on the ground at the airport—everywhere, that is, except in the loading and unloading areas.

Aerodrome controllers accept incoming planes from controllers in the control centres mentioned earlier and make sure that they are spaced out at safe intervals as they queue to land.

Air traffic control assistant

Working alongside the controllers at the control centres are the air traffic control assistants. Their duties include checking flight plans, passing on information to other control centres, supplying weather, flight and navigation information to pilots, and keeping a record of aircraft movements. In some cases there are chances of promotion to air traffic controllers but this is by no means automatic.

Emergency services

Military controllers sit alongside civilian controllers in most of the big control centres. In Britain, the centres listen all the time for distress calls from either civil or military planes and can fix their position within seconds. The emergency service can then alert the rescue services, including RAF mountain rescue, coastguards and so on, and can ask radar units to keep track of the plane in distress, and help it to the nearest airport.

THE INTERNATIONAL PHONETIC ALPHABET	
A	N
Alfa	November
B	O
Bravo	Oscar
C	P
Charlie	Papa
D	Q
Delta	Quebec
E	R
Echo	Romeo
F	S
Foxtrot	Sierra
G	T
Golf	Tango
H	U
Hotel	Uniform
I	V
India	Victor
J	W
Juliett	Whiskey
K	X
Kilo	X-ray
L	Y
Lima	Yankee
M	Z
Mike	Zulu

On the apron

After a plane has landed at a big modern airport, the flight crew are told by the controllers in the tower where to turn off the runway and which taxi track to take towards the terminal buildings.

To help the pilots take the right path, a row of green lights sunk into the taxi track chosen by the controllers is switched on. Sometimes you will see an airport car drive out to meet the incoming plane. On its roof it will have a large sign which says 'Follow me'.

Some airports have over 100 parking places or stands, where airliners finish and start journeys, and where the passengers get off and on. On hearing of the approach of a particular flight, the marshalling department at the airport works out which stand is free for the plane. They then tell all the other departments who must know. By the time the plane arrives at the stand, as many as 20 vehicles and 40 airport workers may be waiting to spring into action. One of the first people to arrive on the scene is the marshaller, who is in charge of the whole operation.

The drivers of all the vehicles waiting on the apron will have obtained permission from the control tower first before proceeding to the plane. Every car, truck or bus is fitted with two-way radio so that the drivers are in continual contact with a ground controller.

The plane comes to a halt and chocks, metal blocks which stop the plane moving on the ground, are placed in front of the wheels. Next the generator truck is plugged in to the plane. Normally the power for a plane's lighting system and all the other electrical circuits is provided by its engines. But when the engines are switched off, electricity is supplied by a motor driven generator mounted on a trailer.

While buses whisk passengers away to the terminal, Customs officers board the plane. Their job is to check the duty-free goods and lock the bars. This is to make sure that no tax-free drinks can be sold until the plane is in the air again.

When the Customs officers have finished, they leave the way clear for the cleaners, caterers, maintenance engineers and all the other workers involved in preparing the plane for its next flight.

▲ At Dulles Airport, Washington, passengers are taken to the airliners from the terminal in a fleet of 'mobile lounges'. They are like huge buses. Drivers raise the body level with the door of the plane and passengers walk on board through a corridor which looks like a giant concertina.

◄ A British Airways Concorde at Heathrow Airport, London, is surrounded by a fleet of trucks. Each one has a different job—refuelling, taking off luggage, bringing new catering supplies —which must be completed before another flight can start. Under Concorde's nose is a powerful tug which will push it away from the terminal at departure time.

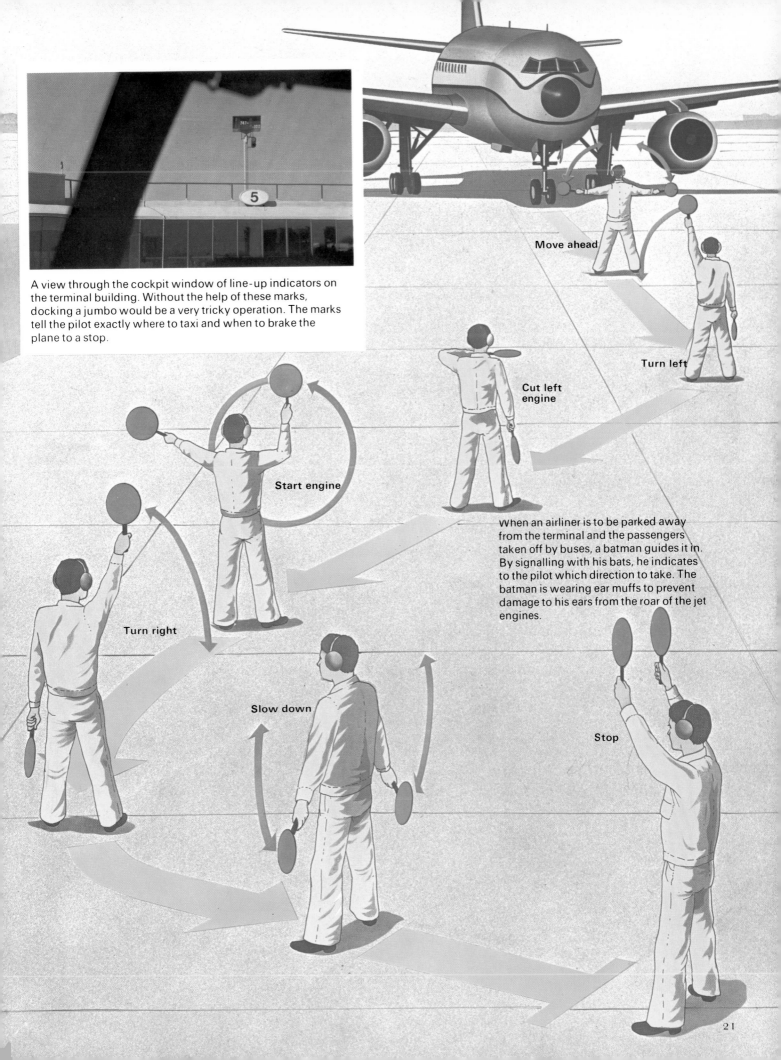

A view through the cockpit window of line-up indicators on the terminal building. Without the help of these marks, docking a jumbo would be a very tricky operation. The marks tell the pilot exactly where to taxi and when to brake the plane to a stop.

Move ahead

Turn left

Cut left engine

Start engine

Turn right

Slow down

When an airliner is to be parked away from the terminal and the passengers taken off by buses, a batman guides it in. By signalling with his bats, he indicates to the pilot which direction to take. The batman is wearing ear muffs to prevent damage to his ears from the roar of the jet engines.

Stop

A quick turnround

▶ **12.00** A short haul jet arrives at the airport and must be ready to fly again in only 60 minutes. Passengers leave immediately and pilots report any defects to engineers.

◀ **12.02** New air crew checks in.

▼ **12.08** The catering van arrives, baggage is unloaded, cabin cleaning begins and pilots leave the plane after a final word with the engineer.

As soon as the passengers and their baggage have been unloaded, the plane is made ready for its next flight. Airlines want their airliners to be on the ground for as short a time as possible, for they only make money when they are flying.

Completing a turnround between flights on a jumbo jet is a massive operation involving up to 100 workers. It is usually completed in two hours. On smaller planes carrying smaller loads and fewer passengers, the job can take as little as half an hour.

Among the first workers to go on board are the cleaners. After a long flight with 300 people on board, the inside of a jumbo will be in a terrible mess. Up to half a ton of rubbish is often removed.

There are 15 toilets on a jumbo, all of which have to be emptied, cleaned and restocked. They are emptied automatically by a special truck. Carpets throughout all the cabins are vacuum-cleaned and then covered so that they do not become dirty before the next flight. Seats are also vacuumed, tables, cabin walls and windows wiped, and head-rest covers replaced.

Meanwhile another gang is busy removing the debris of meals and drinks from the jumbo's galleys. Fresh food is brought on board and packed away. For a long flight with 300 passengers there will be as many as 1,000 separate meals, in addition to many litres of coffee, tea, beers, wines and spirits.

▼ **12.20** Freight unloading and loading is in progress.

Underneath the plane, workers are unloading up to 17 tons of cargo from the holds beneath the floor of the passenger cabin and replacing it with a fresh load.

At the same time men employed by the oil companies are refuelling the plane, either from road tankers or, at the most modern airports, from pipes which come out of the ground. Refuelling a plane is a much bigger operation than filling the petrol tank of a car. A jumbo can swallow 178,000 litres of aviation fuel and filling up the tanks can take 20 minutes.

While this is happening, a wide variety of stores is going on board—baby foods, cornflakes, bars of soap, tubes of toothpaste, paper and linen towels, new films for the in-flight cinema show, newspapers, sweets and nuts, needles and thread, and, for the first class cabin, a bowl of fresh roses.

Engineers from the airline which owns the plane put right any minor faults which the pilots have noted during the previous flight. In the cockpit the instruments, radar, radios and electrical systems are checked. Another engineer checks the fittings in the cabin. He makes sure that the reading lights for every seat are working, checks that the mechanism which enables passengers to recline their seats is in order, and that the oxygen, air-conditioning and refrigeration systems are working properly.

Routine maintenance checks are carried out on the plane and its engines to a plan laid down by the airline. Each job is carefully ticked off on a list when it is completed. Oil levels are checked, as are the pressures in the tyres on all 18 wheels.

Then after a final shine has been given to the cockpit windows, the ground engineer in charge will say that he is satisfied that the plane is ready for its next flight. Only then is the signal given to allow the next batch of passengers to start going on board.

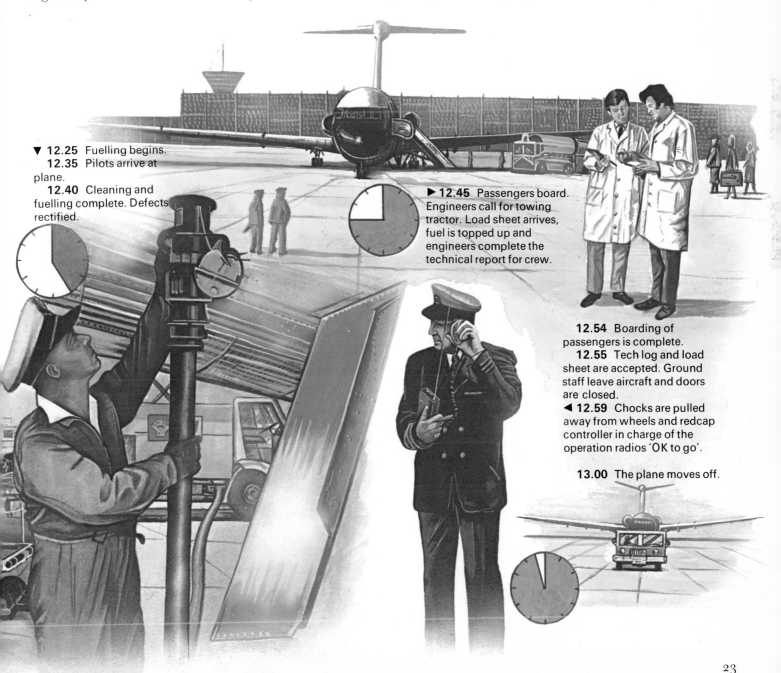

▼ **12.25** Fuelling begins.
12.35 Pilots arrive at plane.
12.40 Cleaning and fuelling complete. Defects rectified.

▶ **12.45** Passengers board. Engineers call for towing tractor. Load sheet arrives, fuel is topped up and engineers complete the technical report for crew.

12.54 Boarding of passengers is complete.
12.55 Tech log and load sheet are accepted. Ground staff leave aircraft and doors are closed.
◀ **12.59** Chocks are pulled away from wheels and redcap controller in charge of the operation radios 'OK to go'.

13.00 The plane moves off.

In the maintenance hangar

On the outskirts of every airport there are a number of enormous hangars which are bustling with activity 24 hours a day. These are the engineering bases where the airlines keep their planes in top flying condition. Employed in them are hundreds of highly skilled engineers who between them look after every one of the thousands of parts which go to make up a modern airliner.

Just occasionally a plane has to be taken into the base for emergency repairs, for example if one of its engines is damaged by stones blown up off the runway as it is taking off or landing. But generally the planes go in for maintenance to a carefully prepared plan. The longer they have been flying, the more work they have done on them.

In the case of Concorde, for example, each plane is towed into the base after every 25 flying hours, when the four engines are inspected and various other routine jobs carried out. After 75 flying hours the inspection gets more detailed and after 150 hours more detailed still. After 720 hours the inspection includes items such as the safety equipment, the hydraulics and lubrication systems, the electrical systems, the flying control systems, the engines and the instruments. The final stage is always a thorough clean. Aircraft are kept spotlessly clean outside as a coating of dirt would slow them down so that far more fuel would be used than is necessary. These inspections usually take one or two days.

Every three or four years all planes are grounded for a couple of weeks and completely stripped down and overhauled. Every possible component is tested and inspected. X-rays are used to test the condition of inaccessible parts of the plane.

Modern airliners are designed to make servicing and repairs as quick and easy as possible. Airliners such as Concorde have among their equipment a number of 'black boxes'. These contain advanced electronics which control such things as the navigation systems and the doors which open and close to allow the right amount of air into the engines.

If something goes wrong inside one of these black boxes, it is not necessary for the engineers to open it and attempt repairs on the spot. They simply disconnect the box and connect up a new one. The faulty unit is then removed to the repair shops and mended without the plane being delayed.

Such shortcuts to maintenance are invaluable as every hour a plane is out of service it is losing the airline money. Service checks on all planes are carried out as quickly and efficiently as possible. There must be no delay because of missing parts; no workers standing idle waiting for someone else to complete a task before they can start on their own work. All maintenance is carried out to a carefully planned schedule, each stage of which is ticked off on job cards on completion and double checked by a foreman.

▲ A jumbo jet gets a wash and brush up.

◄ Computers are an invaluable aid to the efficient running of an engineering base. They can find faults and keep track of the thousands of spare parts in store.

▲ A mechanic works on an undercarriage leg. Airliner undercarriages take a lot of punishment and have to be checked regularly.

◄ TWA engineers carry out maintenance on a jet engine. All big airlines have their own engine engineering bases staffed by specialists.

▼ Working on the flight deck of an airliner are two of the most specialized staff in the airline engineering team. They are checking the highly-complicated electronics and instrument systems which the pilots use to find their way through the skies. Their job is vital, for a fault in one dial could keep the plane grounded.

Working with planes

For every one airport worker in the public eye, there must be another half dozen whom the public never see. These are the engineers, the loaders, the men who refuel the planes, the cargo-handlers and the drivers. Although they work behind the scenes, their jobs are vital to the smooth and safe running of airports and the airlines which use them.

Engineer

Aeronautical engineers work in a number of different places. They can be employed in the industry which makes aircraft or equipment for aircraft, at government establishments doing research into aviation, by companies which specialize in maintenance and overhaul, or by airlines.

An engineer working for an airline will almost certainly work at an airport. His duties will take him either to the airline's engineering base or to the planes waiting in between flights at the passenger or cargo terminals.

There are also job opportunities overseas, as every airline with international routes keeps engineers based at its foreign stations. In the case of large airlines, they have small engineering bases at their more important points abroad where quite major tasks on their planes can be carried out.

At the main engineering base on the home airport the airliners come in for maintenance to a carefully-arranged schedule. There are a series of different checks which have to be carried out at regular intervals. A plane can be in the hangar from a few hours to several days, depending on which of these checks is being carried out.

At the terminals the engineers are engaged in routine checks to make sure the planes are fit to fly their next service, and also in 'trouble shooting'—putting right minor faults which have been reported by the pilots or flight engineer during the flight that has just finished.

In each of these main areas of work the engineers will be specialists in different fields—airframes, engines, electronics, radio and radar, and so on. At the engineering base there are opportunities for a wide range of specialized jobs, including sheet metal work, carpentry, painting and upholstery.

Every big airline is constantly trying to improve the performance of its planes, both from the safety and money-saving points of view. A number of engineers will therefore be engaged on research and development projects. Another highly-specialized and skilled job is that of the instrument worker, who maintains the extremely complicated series of clocks, dials and gauges which the pilots use to help them fly the planes.

Like almost all other airport personnel, engineers have to work shifts, often at nights and at weekends. The work can be demanding and can require great concentration and attention to detail. A careless mistake could endanger the lives of hundreds of passengers.

The main way of entering the profession is through an apprenticeship. Many of the bigger airlines, and the specialist aircraft overhaul firms have their own apprenticeship schemes, taking young men and women on for four-year courses.

Through such courses the students become specialists in one or more of the branches mentioned above. There are also opportunities for further training, and degree courses to Bachelor of Science standard are often available.

Entry into aeronautical engineering is also possible through a university course. In the case of British Airways, technical training takes place for the first 18 months at its apprentice training school at Heathrow Airport and is linked closely with studies at college. The remaining year of the apprenticeship is completed in the hangars, maintenance workshops, and development and planning departments of the airline.

Opportunities for advancement in engineering are good. Many apprentices go on later in their careers to become station engineers, simulator engineers, engineering instructors and flight engineers.

Loader

Loaders are employed by the airline to load and unload passenger baggage and cargo in the holds of their planes. Although more mechanized equipment is being introduced by the airlines, this is a tough and demanding job, requiring strength and physical fitness. Training is given in the use of the mechanical handling equipment.

Driver

Airports are enormous places—the road round the outside of Dallas/Fort Worth, Texas, for example, runs for nearly 40 kilometres—and all companies with aviation business maintain fleets of ground vehicles. Job opportunities for drivers at airports are therefore many and varied, ranging from heavy goods vehicle drivers to chauffeurs for the cars of the executives.

There are also a whole range of specialist vehicles at airports. These range from trucks with sets of steps on their back which are run up to the doors of planes on some occasions so that the passengers can disembark, to large and very powerful tractors capable of towing the biggest jet with a full load of passengers and freight.

Vehicles on the runways must obviously be very carefully monitored and drivers must learn to follow the instructions given to them by ground control at all times.

► A diagram of a typical modern jet with the position of the fuel tanks shown in blue.

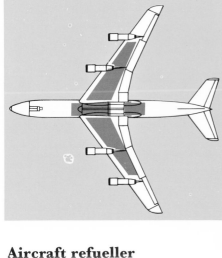

Cleaner

The standard of cleanliness of a plane's cabin makes an immediate impression on an airline's passengers. If a passenger coming on board finds the plane dirty, he may well decide not to travel with that airline again. The cleaners have an important job to do, even though at times it is not very pleasant. They must be prepared to work quickly and efficiently as a plane must spend as short a time as possible on the tarmac between flights. Cleaners are normally employed by outside firms who have contracts with the airlines.

Aircraft refueller

The refuellers have a highly responsible job on the airport. They drive the enormous fuel tankers owned by the various oil companies up to the planes, and then connect them up with the fuel tanks of the aircraft so that the precise amount of fuel asked for by the pilots is piped on board. A heavy goods vehicle driving licence, and a detailed knowledge of the specialist equipment carried on the tankers and the airliners is vital. Refuellers are employed by the oil companies.

Needless to say, there is no smoking allowed on this job. The aircraft refueller is carefully instructed in the safety precautions covering his highly dangerous load, and in the steps to be taken in an emergency.

▲ These two cheerful cooks prepare hundreds of airline meals a day. These are then loaded onto the galleys of aircraft, ready to be served up in minutes by the cabin crew.

► Every plane gets a thorough cleaning between each flight.

◄ Engineering apprentices receive instruction inside a demonstration fuselage, to show them how a modern airliner is built. They learn about the 'fail-safe' design of a plane, which means that if one part fails, another takes the strain.

▼ Driving the tug which pulls a jumbo jet worth perhaps £10 million is a highly responsible job.

Safety first!

Airport authorities have tried many ways of scaring birds from runways. Falcons are used to chase them away, the rubbish tips where they feed are filled in, the grass is left long so they cannot land, blank shots are fired, the sounds of birds of prey are broadcast. And at one airport, a man has been trained to act like a hawk! But still the birds come . . . !

▲ Snow and ice can be extremely hazardous when planes are taking off and landing and so heavy equipment is kept specially to shift it off runways and taxiways.

◄ No airport is allowed to operate without firemen who stay on call 24 hours a day. Here firemen at Heathrow hose down a Concorde after smoke had come from an engine.

Flying is one of the safest forms of transport known to man. This is not mere chance, but because flight safety regulations and procedures are extremely thorough. Planes are regularly serviced, runways and lighting systems carefully maintained, and emergency services on hand at airports at all times. But one of the most important factors is the design of the plane itself.

Airliners are extremely tough and made to a very high engineering standard. Most of them have a flying life of at least 15 years. Before a new type of airliner is put into production three prototypes are usually made. Two of these are flown by test pilots.

The third prototype is 'tested to destruction'. It is put into a sort of torture chamber where heavy weights are hung on its wings and then jacked up and down. These movements are similar to those which the plane makes when it is actually flying. The jacks torture the test plane hundreds of thousands of times, until the wing does at last crack. The aircraft designers can then work out how many years it would be before the plane is likely to break while in the air. This must be at a point in time which the plane will never actually reach in its flying life.

Jet engines too are tested to destruction. They are run at full power for thousands of hours to make sure that they are safe in flight. A particular hazard for jet engines is bird strike damage. A jet engine sucks in the enormous amounts of air which it needs through fan blades which go round at great speed. To make sure that these fan blades will not snap if a large bird flies into them, the carcasses of dead chickens are fired into them at the engine factory.

In spite of all the tests which are carried out on planes, parts of them do occasionally break. But although this is serious, such an accident does not necessarily lead to a crash.

Aircraft designers make sure that planes are built to a 'fail-safe' plan. If one part of the structure of the fuselage, or the wings, or the tail breaks, other parts of the plane's structure can carry the strain—at least until the plane lands and can be repaired.

If an inspection shows that the part has broken through a manufacturing fault, similar parts on all other planes in the airline will be replaced at once. And a warning will be flashed to other airlines all over the world using similar aircraft, telling them exactly what has happened. In serious cases, every plane of the same type will be ordered to stay on the ground by the aviation authorities until they have discovered exactly what went wrong.

Take-off and landing are potentially the most dangerous parts of a flight so keeping the runways clear at all times is vital. Sometimes bits fall from airliners as they take off or land. If another plane struck the obstacle, a tyre could burst and cause an accident. A team of men drive up and down the runways looking for rubbish and the runways are also vacuum-cleaned regularly.

▼ A VC 10 airliner in a 'torture chamber' has heavy loads put on it thousands of times to make sure it is strong enough to fly safely. The tests cleared the plane for a flying life of up to 25 years.

Air crash!

Mayday, Mayday, Mayday! The air traffic controller picks up the distress call from a pilot who is coming in to land with an engine on fire. Action stations! The controller immediately alerts the police, the fire brigade and the ambulance service who rush to the scene.

Air traffic controllers then clear the way for the damaged plane to land by alerting all other planes in the area to keep off the approach. They have to direct the plane down the fastest possible approach and at the same time make sure all the other planes are flying safe courses.

Meanwhile the firemen have rushed to the runway in special airport fire engines with speeds matching those of sports cars. Fire is a particular danger in air crashes. It is vital that the flames are put out before they reach the plane's fuel tanks. So before the plane lands, firemen lay special foam on the runway to lessen the risk of fire spreading from the engine to the tanks.

By the time the plane comes in to land, all the emergency services are on hand to get the passengers and crew to safety. The passengers escape down the emergency chutes and are taken off in ambulances to be treated for shock and minor injuries. No one is seriously hurt.

Of course not all incidents are dealt with so successfully. When a plane falls to earth from high altitude there is obviously nothing that can be done for the passengers. The most common cause for such crashes is mid-air collisions when two planes have struck each other in flight. Planes fly at such speeds that by the time a pilot sees another plane in his path, it could already be too late for him to take avoiding action.

But the most common causes of loss of life in aviation are accidents which occur either on take-off or landing. On take-off there is the danger of engines failing. Sometimes while trying to land, the crew have misjudged and put the plane down short of the runway. When the crash is at the airport there are often survivors. Every airport has a carefully worked-out emergency plan which can be put into operation at a moment's notice and the rescue services are trained to move at great speed.

On average some 1000 people are killed each year in airliner accidents. This is a terrible waste of life but it is a tiny proportion of the total number of over 600 million passengers who fly with the airlines of the world each year.

Experts have worked out that people have less chance of being killed or injured while flying than they have on almost any type of surface transport.

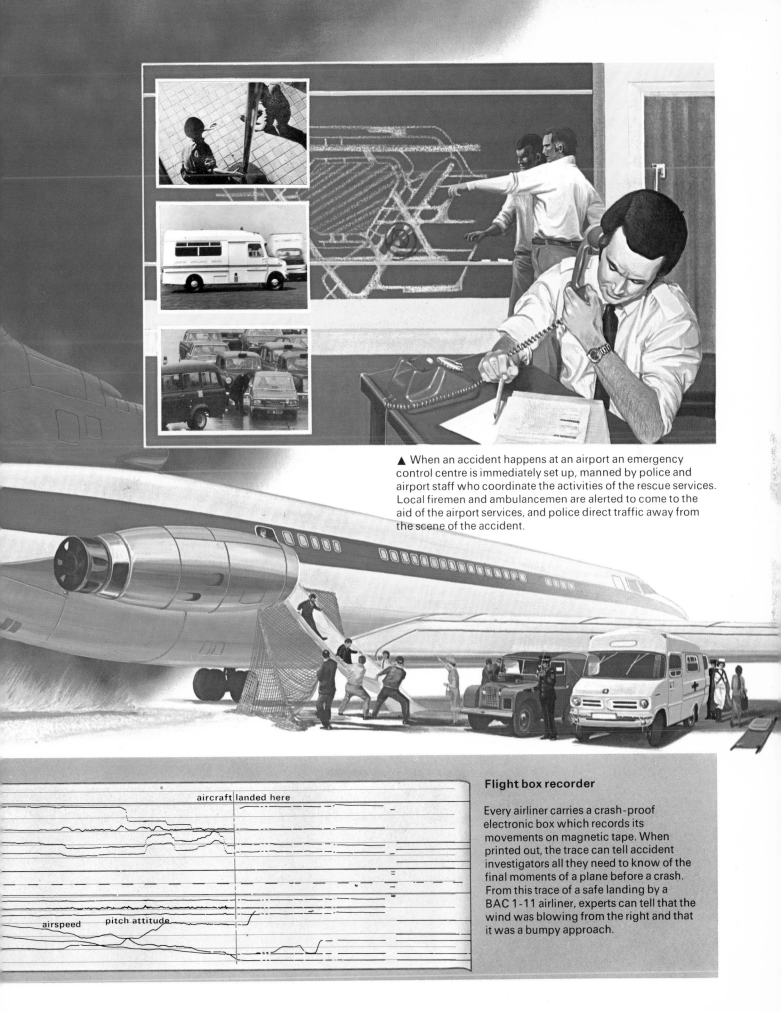

▲ When an accident happens at an airport an emergency control centre is immediately set up, manned by police and airport staff who coordinate the activities of the rescue services. Local firemen and ambulancemen are alerted to come to the aid of the airport services, and police direct traffic away from the scene of the accident.

aircraft landed here

airspeed   pitch attitude

Flight box recorder

Every airliner carries a crash-proof electronic box which records its movements on magnetic tape. When printed out, the trace can tell accident investigators all they need to know of the final moments of a plane before a crash. From this trace of a safe landing by a BAC 1-11 airliner, experts can tell that the wind was blowing from the right and that it was a bumpy approach.

Security and safety services

By law an airport cannot be open for flying unless there are firemen on duty ready to move to the rescue of trapped passengers in a matter of seconds in the event of a crash. The firemen always hit the headlines, but there are many other people in the security and safety services at airports who spend their days waiting for trouble, or doing routine checks to see that trouble does not happen.

Firemen

Firemen are normally employed by the authority which runs the airport. Entrants have to be young and in very good physical condition. Training is given at specialist aviation fire schools where they learn to deal efficiently with the many different types of emergency that can occur at airports.

The fire station is usually situated near the control tower so that all of the runways on which accidents might happen are within easy reach. But life for the airport firemen is by no means all sensational rescues. They deal also with routine tasks, such as putting out small fires in offices, and mopping up spilled fuel around the planes.

▶ Fire services at airports are constantly ready for emergencies. In a training session, men wearing asbestos suits pour foam on to a wreck set ablaze on purpose.

▼ A real disaster. French firemen work in the wreck of a Boeing 707. A careless smoker caused the blaze.

Ambulancemen

Like the firemen, ambulancemen are always prepared for large-scale emergencies, but they spend most of their time dealing with routine cases. With 20 million passengers passing through a big airport each year, and some 50,000 people working there, it is inevitable that there will be

regular calls to attend cases of heart attacks, broken limbs, and similar everyday occurrences.

Although they have sick rooms, airports do not have their own hospitals. Cases are taken to specialist units in the towns and cities nearby. In a major emergency involving a plane and possibly hundreds of people, these hospitals would send in their ambulances and medical staffs to help those services that are based on the airport.

Doctors and nurses

Every major airport has its own team of doctors and nurses who, like the ambulancemen, move into their jobs through the usual entry channels in the medical profession. Some will be employed by the airport authority, some by government health authorities, and some by the big airlines who have their bases on or near the airport.

The work of the medical staff falls into two main categories. Firstly, they attend to the health needs of passengers and airline and airport staff. Secondly they have the important task of checking that incoming passengers do not bring disease into the country by making sure that they have had the necessary vaccinations.

Security officers

Security officers are normally employed by outside contractors. There are not such rigid age rules for joining as there are in the police force. But as with the police, all recruits are carefully vetted to make sure they have no criminal record and are completely trustworthy.

A major part of their job is to guard airport buildings and installations, often with the help of trained guard dogs. The freight warehouses in particular usually contain goods worth many millions of pounds, and are frequently the target for gangs of thieves.

Security officers are also stationed at gates to every entrance from the landside of an airport, where passengers and cars are allowed to move freely, to the airside, where the planes are parked. They make sure that no unauthorised person is able to go near the aircraft and perhaps tamper with them.

Another important task is to frisk passengers boarding planes to check that they are not carrying any weapons that might be used in a mid-air hijacking.

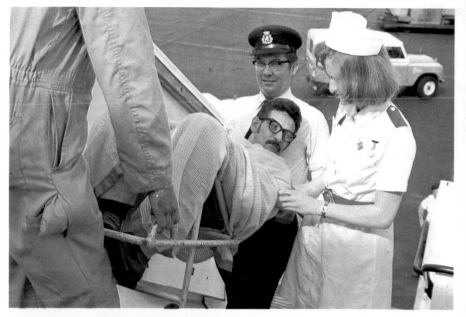

▲ Airport medical staff are trained for emergencies, but also deal with routine tasks. Here an invalid on a stretcher is helped on board an airliner.

◄ Before boarding planes, all passengers are frisked for weapons which might be used in a hijacking.

Police

If an airport is like a medium-sized town, then it must have its police force to keep the traffic moving, prevent crime, and to carry out the 101 other jobs which the police do for the community. Some airports have their own separate police force. Others, like Heathrow, London, have officers who are part of the force of the city which the airport serves.

Every airport has its own police station. Some of the officers who are based there wear ordinary civilian clothes, mingling with the passengers and the staff in their efforts to reduce crime.

At almost all airports throughout the world, at least some of the police carry guns. This is necessary as airports have become the targets for many attacks in the past few years by terrorist groups. Each airport police force has a well-rehearsed emergency plan, under which units of the army would be called in if such a terrorist attack took place.

Men and women go through the normal police training before they are drafted to work at an airport. Once there they will pick up a great deal of specialized knowledge on aviation and the types of crimes that the business attracts. Traffic congestion is usually a great problem, but many airports have a force of traffic wardens to back up the police in controlling the traffic flow.

▲ A French security officer searches a passenger's luggage for weapons. Airlines fight a constant war against piracy attempts.

Cargo loading

Cargo on board the first ever international air service in 1919 was a packet of newspapers, two dead birds for somebody's lunch and a pot of cream. Today a jumbo jet can carry 100 tons of freight on each flight—anything from a midget submarine to a string of racehorses.

Air freight is now an important part of every airline's activity. Every big airport has its own cargo 'village' where the goods are received, stored and then despatched.

Until fairly recently most heavy cargo was sent by sea, road or rail. Small items worth a lot of money such as diamonds, or urgently needed medicines and hospital supplies, were sent by air. Air freight was also used to send goods which were likely to go out of fashion quickly, such as pop records and clothes. But with today's bigger, more powerful planes, heavy items ranging from bags of cement to factory machinery, from prefabricated buildings to dismantled cars, are now shipped regularly by air.

Although most airlines have planes which carry nothing but freight, the majority of cargo is still carried in the underfloor holds on passenger services.

In the jumbo jets and airbuses the freight is not thrown into the holds in a jumble. It is either loaded in containers or stacked on pallets, wooden trays which act as a base onto which the freight is tied. The pallets and containers are shifted into place in the holds on a series of miniature rail lines which are worked by one operator.

It is absolutely vital that cargo is loaded evenly in an airliner. If too much was placed in either the nose or the tail the aircraft would be nose or tail heavy. This would affect the way the plane flew, causing it to use more fuel. If the weight distribution was very unbalanced, the plane could even be unsafe. So cargo has to be loaded according to a very carefully worked out plan.

An all-cargo Boeing 707 for example can carry up to 40 tons. The freight is distributed through the cabin on 13 pallets, each of which is weighed carefully before it is put on to the aircraft. Then, with the help of a computer, a loadmaster allocates each pallet a place in the plane, depending on its weight and also its bulk. Each aircraft has a known centre of gravity—the point at which it would balance like a seesaw—and the aim is to distribute the weight evenly around this point. It is a very delicate operation. Even the addition of an extra radio in the cockpit would upset the balance. The trick of the trade is to finish up with the aircraft very slightly tail heavy, as it flies more efficiently in this attitude.

Working in the cargo department at an airport can be hard work. For although the bigger airlines have installed machines which handle these goods mechanically, much is still shifted by muscle-power.

◄ The computer is an invaluable aid to this worker, who is using it to direct cases being loaded into containers. Computers and mechanical handling devices are being used more and more in the cargo industry.

▲ In the new wide-bodied airliners, cargo is no longer loaded one piece at a time but is packed in containers, shaped to fit the planes. These are then lifted on board, saving time and space—both precious in the airline world.

▲ Shipping livestock is now big business for the airlines. These three horses have just crossed the Atlantic in a jumbo freighter, looked after all the way by a team of grooms who fed and watered them.

▶ Among the 100 tons of cargo in this jumbo is another aircraft—slightly smaller in size!

▼ Porsche racing cars are loaded in a jumbo freighter. The loaders can shift them from one rail to another at the touch of a switch.

The passengers disembark

To passengers stepping off a plane, especially if it is in a foreign country, the modern airport can seem a huge and bewildering place. So the people who run airports take great care to provide a lot of very clear signs relying on pictures rather than words, showing where they have to go.

Passengers go first to immigration control, where officials inspect the papers of everybody wanting to enter the country. The immigration officers come into contact with people all over the world, and so knowledge of foreign languages is obviously very useful. If an arriving passenger does not have the right papers, the immigration officers can refuse him entry and put him back on a plane to the country from which he has flown.

If passengers have come from countries where there are known to be active diseases, they will have to pass through health control. There, doctors and nurses make sure that they have had the correct vaccinations and innoculations which will prevent them from bringing disease into the country. If they have not, they have to be 'jabbed' on the spot.

Having passed through these checks, the passengers then move on to the hall where they collect their luggage which they last saw when they checked in at the departure airport.

Waiting for one's luggage to appear can be an anxious moment—there is always the thought that perhaps it was never put on the plane. But this happens fairly rarely. Of the 40 million pieces of baggage passing through Heathrow Airport each year, around 80,000 can be expected to go astray. Most of it turns up eventually but not before the passenger has suffered a great deal of inconvenience.

After collecting their luggage, passengers go straight to Customs control. Once through the Customs check, they are free to leave the airport and go by bus, taxi, car or train to their homes or hotels. 'Interlining' or transit passengers—those who arrive by air and are going on to another international flight—do not go through any of these checks but are kept in a separate waiting room until their onward flight is ready to depart.

▲ Before they can enter the country, all passengers must have their passports checked at the immigration desks. Immigration officers keep lists of people who are not to be allowed in and must spot these 'undesirables'. They keep a sharp look-out for forged documents.

► A health control officer examines the papers of incoming passengers to check that they have had any necessary vaccinations or inoculations, and make sure that there is no danger of them bringing disease into the country.

| 1 Transit | 2 Waiting lounge | 3 Information | 4 Car rental | 5 Baggage claim | 6 Emergency telephone | 7 Passport control | 8 Toilets |

▲ Jimmy Carter, President of the United States, arrives at the airport in the presidential Boeing 707. VIPs do not have to wait with the other passengers to disembark. They receive special quick Customs clearance and baggage handling. Private rooms are set aside at airports for newspaper and television journalists to interview them.

▼ These chimps get special treatment too! Most large modern airports have animal hostels where animals can stay in between flights or while waiting for collection by their owners. The hostels have facilities for looking after anything from a stick insect to an elephant. They are staffed by fully qualified veterinary doctors and nurses.

▼ Passenger baggage is unloaded from the planes and taken by truck to carousels. These are belts which move round and round. Passengers pick up their bags from them.

Customs control

'Customs £1 million drug haul at airport'. Headlines such as this make the Customs officer's job seem very glamorous. But such incidents do not happen every day. Most of the time is spent in routine checking and for days on end the Customs officer may seize nothing more exciting than a few bottles of whisky or a few boxes of cigars.

Not all Customs officers are in the public eye. Hundreds are employed in the cargo warehouses of the airlines. Their job is to work out how much duty, or tax, must be paid on every item that passes through. At the same time they must be on the lookout for smuggled goods such as drugs and diamonds. In the warehouse they are under a great deal of pressure. The companies to which the goods have been sent are anxious to have them cleared by the Customs as soon as possible, so that they can move them out of the warehouse and into their shops and factories.

In the passenger area of the airport, the officers are on constant alert as arriving passengers pass through with their luggage. At most airports today passengers can choose whether to go through one of two channels, the red or the green. Everybody is allowed to bring into the country a limited amount of goods, such as alcohol, cigarettes and perfumes, on which they have not paid taxes. The green channel is for those who are within the limit and who have nothing to declare. The red channel

▲ Customs officers have a fund of stories about smugglers they have caught: 'innocent' little old ladies smuggling in vast quantities of alcohol and cigarettes; youths hiding drugs in their shoes; women trying to smuggle in new fur coats, with watches strapped to their legs; even men smuggling diamonds in cricket stumps! But no one can escape the watchful eye of a Customs officer . . . or can they?!

▶ Customs officers carry out random searches on passengers going through the green channel.

is for those who have gone over the limit and who want to declare it and pay duty.

In the red channel, the Customs officers work out how much duty is owing and accept payment. In the green channel they stop a certain number of those passing through and ask them to open their bags and cases. If they are found to be over the limit, they are in trouble and could end up in court.

Customs officers must be good judges of character and have acute powers of detection, so that they can spot from among thousands of passengers who pass before them those who are trying to break the law. Passengers with shifty eyes, who talk too much and who perspire a lot are often suspect. But even when they have stopped a suspicious-looking character, the officers have to be clever to find the contraband. Suitcases with false bottoms and shoes with hollowed-out heels are still popular hiding places but passengers think up new tricks all the time.

As Customs officers have to deal with people in often trying circumstances, they need to keep calm and patient. It is also helpful if they know at least one foreign language. And of course it is no nine-to-five job. Flights arrive at any time of the day and night, and so Customs officers work in shifts. They are expected to be just as alert at three o'clock in the morning as they are in the middle of the day.

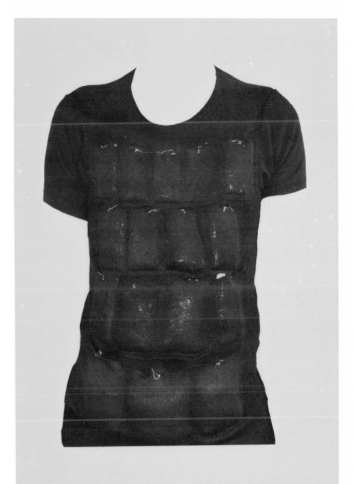

Smugglers go to enormous pains to hide their booty. One had a shirt specially made with pockets in which he tried to bring in drugs worth a fortune. Suspicious Customs officers asked him to take off his jacket, and foiled his plan.

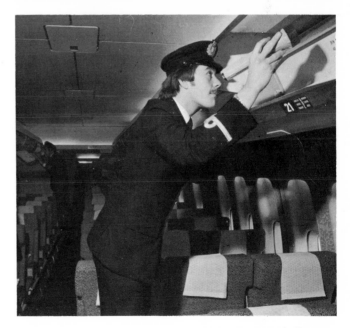

▲ Customs officers do not only work in the Customs hall at airports. Here one seaches an aircraft for contraband such as cocaine.

Security alert

'There is a bomb aboard your flight XYZ bound for Paris timed to go off 20 minutes after take off.' The caller to the airline's head office does not give any name, and rings off immediately.

The airlines are used to such calls. They probably receive at least one each week, and 999 times out of every thousand they are hoaxes. Yet they must take every call seriously. A carefully thought-out plan is put into action at once.

If the plane has just taken off, the pilots are told to return to the airport immediately. The passengers and crew then leave the plane without delay.

Security men take every piece of cargo and baggage off the aircraft. With dogs trained to sniff out explosives, they carry out a thorough search of the plane. Meanwhile the passengers are asked to identify their own baggage. If any bag remains unclaimed, it is taken to a remote corner of the airport and opened by a bomb-disposal expert.

Every item of cargo is searched. If, as usually happens, no bomb is found, the passengers are allowed to board again and the flight leaves once more. It takes about three hours to search a plane carrying 150 people and costs the airline many hundreds of pounds.

But not all security alarms prove groundless. Over the past few years safety in the air has been severely threatened by hijackers. By smuggling weapons on board, they manage to hold the planes up and force the pilots to fly them to their chosen destination. Usually the hijackers are members of political organizations who want to be taken to a country friendly to their cause. The resulting publicity draws world-wide attention to their organization.

Most of these hijackings have succeeded, for almost all the pilots have instructions not to resist. Fights inside airliners, with shots being fired or even bombs exploding, could endanger the safety of the passengers.

Precautions against these pirates of the air cost airports and airlines hundreds of millions of pounds each year. Airports have to employ small armies of security guards to check the passengers and their luggage. Every handbag carried by every traveller must be searched or put through an X-ray machine. And all passengers are frisked or pass through a metal detector to make sure they are not concealing weapons on their person. Thanks to these anti-terrorist measures, the authorities are managing to keep down the number of hijackings.

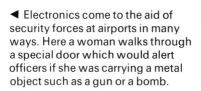

▲ When security fails . . . in 1970 hijackers blew up a VC 10 at Dawson's Field, Amman.

◄ Armoured cars patrol the airport at Munich as efforts are stepped up to prevent aircraft being hijacked.

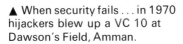

▼ French airport police at Orly, Paris, are equipped with an electronic device for checking passports. The papers are fed in and are transmitted at once to the Ministry of the Interior where they can be checked against a list of 'undesirables' kept there.

◄ Electronics come to the aid of security forces at airports in many ways. Here a woman walks through a special door which would alert officers if she was carrying a metal object such as a gun or a bomb.

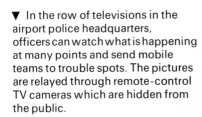

▼ In the row of televisions in the airport police headquarters, officers can watch what is happening at many points and send mobile teams to trouble spots. The pictures are relayed through remote-control TV cameras which are hidden from the public.

Running an airport

At all large airports there are thousands of people working behind the scenes whom the public never see. Yet without administrators, computer operators, caterers, weathermen and a host of others, the complex workings of an airport would quickly grind to a halt. Although some of the jobs described below may be fairly routine ones, they bring the satisfaction of being an important part of an exciting and dynamic organization.

Airport manager

The man with the most important job at any airport is the airport manager. It is his responsibility to see that the million-and-one different operations going on at an airport run smoothly. He is in overall control of the administration and must keep an eye on the shops, the caterers and the airlines operating at the airport. If there are any complaints from passengers about the airport's facilities the manager will be expected to handle them. As well as dealing with everyday problems as they arise, he must also think ahead, by planning new buildings and runways for the future. And in an emergency on airport territory he will be expected to be on hand at all times to coordinate activity.

Administrators

The men and women who run airports are called administrators. Administration covers a wide range of jobs: planners whose task it is to forecast what size the airport needs to be in the future; accountants; people who negotiate contracts with suppliers, shops and airlines; and personnel officers who oversee the recruitment of staff.

Other people are needed in the departments dealing with industrial relations, staff training, organization and methods (which looks for ways of doing jobs better and more cheaply), building design, engineering, estates surveying and valuing, and operational safety (dealing with runways, taxiways and aircraft parking areas). A few airport authorities sell their knowledge abroad to countries who want to develop their own airport, so that there are occasionally chances to travel.

► At busy airports planes may take off as often as every two minutes. To achieve this requires a great deal of work from flight operations staff, airline staff and a host of other workers behind the scenes.

In addition to the big international airports, all countries have a string of small airports where the staff will be numbered in tens rather than thousands. Many people consider that working in such a place is more interesting than at a large airport. Some airport workers have begun their careers at a small airport and have then moved to a larger one later on.

The administrative section provides jobs for people with a wide range of ability and experience. On the one hand there are many openings for graduates, while for school-leavers some airlines and airport authorities have apprenticeship schemes in commercial subjects which can lead to managerial positions at a later stage.

Caterers

With such enormous numbers of people working at or passing through airports each day, there are obviously many opportunities for those interested in the catering profession. Jobs within the catering trade range from the finance and administration staffs to chefs, from waiters and wine waiters to cafeteria assistants, from cashiers to those who keep the tables cleared and clean.

As with so many airport jobs, the work is 'round-the-clock'. It is split between three main types. There are the industrial canteens, catering for the airport workers.

▲ Working as a waitress in an airport restaurant is often hectic, with meals being served around the clock.

There are the public restaurants catering for passengers, which range from the expensive five-star type to self-service snack bars.

Lastly there is in-flight catering, preparing meals for passengers to eat on the planes. These airline kitchens deal with enormous amounts of food. The British Airways kitchen at Heathrow Airport, London, for example, is staffed by 600 workers, who between them produce 16,000 meals every day and another 11,500 deep-frozen meals each week for despatch to the airline's stations overseas.

Banking

The big banks of any country usually have branches at the main airports. Their main function is to change money into foreign currency for people going abroad, and then to change what is left back again on their return. One of the banks at least remains open right through the night, and so working at an airport bank branch can be a very different life from working at a branch in town.

Finance and purchasing

Someone with a head for figures could find an interesting career working in the finance department of an airline. The work covers dealing with day-to-day income and expenditure, checking and accounting for sales of airline services, and analysing the income from every route which the airline flies. He or she would probably come into contact with people doing similar jobs for many of the other world airlines, as the whole airline industry works very closely, constantly exchanging tickets and passengers.

Shops

All the big airports now have their own shopping centres. These often specialize in the goods for which the country is

famous—Schiphol, the airport of Amsterdam, has an enormous cheese shop, for example. The workers in the shops must expect to meet a wide range of nationalities and languages.

After passing through the immigration check, passengers flying out of the airport can go to the duty-free shop where they can buy goods without the usual tax on them. These shops are normally self-service and the assistants sit at desks rather like those at supermarket check-outs.

▲ Almost every airline in the world has introduced computers in the past few years to help with a wide variety of tasks. There are therefore increasing chances for computer trainees and programmers, the men and women who are responsible for writing instructions which are fed to the computers.

▼ Airports try to cater for every need. At Charles de Gaulle Airport, Paris, you can even have your hair done while waiting for a flight.

Flight operations staff

In the flight operations department of an airline, the employees work closely with the pilots. Their job is to draw up the duty rosters which tell the crews when they will fly and on which routes. They also provide their pilots with all the items of information they need to know before they take off: information such as how many passengers and how much cargo they will have on board, which runway they will use and what weather to expect on route.

▼ The flight operations department is responsible for passing on all weather information to the pilots.

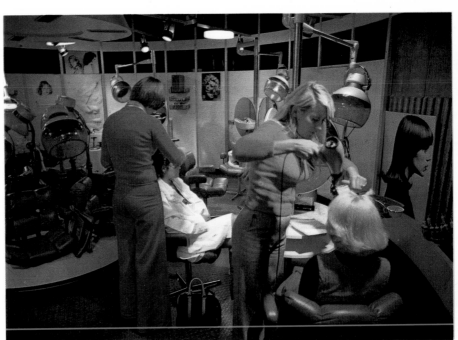

Reference section

General Information

There are a number of different sources which will provide you with valuable advice and details if you are thinking of a career at an airport or in one of the other branches of civil aviation.

Your school guidance counselor and library may have some useful books and pamphlets. If you are interested in working at your local airport in any capacity, you can contact the personnel manager. Another source of local job listings is your area state employment office. Addresses and phone numbers of both airports and employment offices can easily be found in the telephone directory.

The following airline companies are some of the largest employers in the industry.

Trans World Airlines, Inc.
605 Third Ave.
New York, N.Y. 10016

Pan American World Airways, Inc.
Pan Am Bldg.
New York, N.Y. 10017

Eastern Air Lines, Inc.
Miami International Airport
Miami, Fla. 33148

For a complete list of airline companies write to:

Air Transportation Association of America
1709 New York Ave., N.W.
Washington, D.C. 20006

Other sources of employment and information on airport-related careers are the following government agencies:

Office of Personnel
Civil Aeronautics Board (CAB)
1825 Connecticut Ave., N.W.
Washington, D.C. 20428

The CAB regulates the business end of the air transportation industry. The Board employs attorneys, accountants, auditors, economists, air transportation industry analysts and supporting clerical, secretarial and technical staff.

Management Analysis Divn., AMS-500
Office of Management Systems
Federal Aviation Administration (FAA)
800 Independence Ave. S.W.
Washington, D.C. 20591

The FAA issues and enforces safety regulations relating to manufacture, operation and maintenance of aircraft as well as certification of airport personnel and airports. The FAA employs engineers, pilots, air traffic controllers, mechanics and others.

A very useful source of information on airport careers is the U.S. Department of Labor *Occupational Outlook Handbook* Reprint No. 1955-16. It can be obtained by writing your nearest regional office of the Bureau of Labor Statistics. The addresses are:

Boston
1603 Federal Bldg.
Government Center
Boston, Mass. 02203

New York
Suite 3400, 1515 Broadway
New York, N.Y. 10036

Philadelphia
P.O. Box 13309
Philadelphia, Pa. 19101

Atlanta
1371 Peachtree St. N.E.
Atlanta, Ga. 30309

Chicago
9th Floor, Federal Office Bldg.
230 South Dearborn St.
Chicago, Ill. 60604

Dallas
2nd Floor
555 Griffin Square Bldg.
Dallas, Tex. 75202

Kansas City
911 Walnut St.
Kansas City, Mo. 64106

San Francisco
450 Golden Gate Ave., Box 36017
San Francisco, Calif. 94102

American Airlines offers a series of fact sheets listing requirements for flight crews, attendants, mechanics,

▼ A flight engineer makes a last-minute check on the tyres before take-off.

and other airline employees. To request copies write to American Airlines (address listed above).

A color illustrated booklet, *An Introduction to the USAF Academy*, is available from:

Registrar
USAF Academy
Colo. 80840

Qualifications and Training

Flight Attendants

Applicants for jobs as flight attendants must be poised, tactful, and have the ability to deal with the public. Attendants must usually be at least 19 years old, be a high school graduate, and be in excellent health. To work for an international airline it is often necessary that you be able to speak the required foreign language.

Flight attendants generally are given training courses of about five weeks by the airlines. The training includes emergency evacuation procedures and first-aid techniques.

Reservation, Ticket, and Passenger Agents

The people who deal with the passengers, giving them flight information, and reservations and selling them tickets, must have good appearances and speaking voices as well as pleasing personalities.

Airline companies give new employees about four weeks' training—one week in the classroom and three weeks of on-the-job supervised experience.

Many agents belong to unions such as the Air Line Employees Association or the Transport Workers Union of America.

For information regarding the work of reservation, ticket, and passenger agents, write to:

Air Line Employees Association
5600 S. Central Ave.
Chicago, Ill. 60638

Air Traffic Controllers

Air traffic controllers are federal government employees, who work for the Federal Aviation Administration (FAA). Potential candidates for controller jobs must apply to the Federal Civil Service. You can obtain a pamphlet, *Announcement 418*, from your local U.S. Civil Service Job In-formation Center, which is listed in the telephone directory. If there is no listing you can call 800-555-1212 to get the toll-free number of the center for your area. The pamphlet gives information on air controllers' work and directions for applying for training or jobs.

Applicants for training must pass a written test, must have three years of general work experience or four years of college or a combination, must have excellent health, vision correctable to 20/20, a good voice, and a retentive memory. A certain amount of military experience as a pilot or controller can waive the written test.

Applicants receive about sixteen weeks' training at the FAA Academy in Oklahoma City (FAA Academy, P.O. Box 25082, Oklahoma City, Okla. 73125). After about two or three years' experience one is considered a full-fledged controller. Every year controllers must pass a physical examination and twice a year a performance test.

Pilots

There are several different levels of training for pilots, each represented by a certain license. The minimum requirement for a commercial pilot is the FAA commercial pilot's license. To fly in bad weather—by the use of instruments—an additional license is required. Airline pilots need a higher level license—that of FAA flight engineer. Licenses remain valid as long as a pilot can pass the periodic physical and flying exams.

Potential pilots can attend either military or civilian flying schools. Airlines prefer to recruit military-trained pilots because of their experience with jets. College graduates are also given preference. Airlines give additional training courses of several weeks.

To obtain the minimum pilot's license, applicants must be at least 18 years of age and have done at least 250 hours of flying. Excellent health and vision correctable to 20/20 are required. Both a written test and flying tests must be passed.

Airline pilots generally start as flight engineers and can advance to co-pilot, and finally to captain. For captain another license requiring 1500 hours of flying experience during the previous eight years is necessary.

▲ Giving a jumbo a final shine.

For more information on pilot jobs and training write to:

Air Line Pilots Association International
1625 Massachusetts Ave. N.W.
Washington, D.C. 20036

Airplane Mechanics

While most mechanics learn their trade in FAA-certified technical schools or the armed forces, a few high school graduates with mechanical aptitude and course work are accepted for on-the-job training.

After schooling and certain work experience, mechanics are eligible to apply for licensing required for most jobs. There are three types of licenses issued by the FAA:

(1) the powerplant mechanic's license, qualifying you to work only on the engine

(2) the airframe mechanic's license, qualifying you to work on the fuselage, wings, and other parts of the plane

(3) the inspector's license, qualifying you to check work done by other mechanics.

The airframe and powerplant mechanic's license each requires 18 months of work experience, or a combined license can be obtained through 30 months of combined work experience.

To apply for the inspector's license you must have held the combined license for at least three years.

Good physical condition, strength and agility as well as mechanical ability are suitable attributes for airplane mechanics.

For more information contact:
Aviation Maintenance Foundation
P.O. Box 739
Basin, Wyoming 82410

Customs Inspectors

Customs inspectors are federal government employees. For inspector jobs you must first gain a bachelor's degree and three years' work experience preferably related to customs work. Then you must take the Professional and Administrative Career Examination (PACE). If you pass this exam your name is put on a list of eligible candidates to fill vacancies as they occur. Inspectors are given both classroom and on-the-job training in customs laws and procedures.

To apply for a customs job, contact the nearest U.S. Government Job Information Center, listed in your telephone directory.

Airport Management

There is a wide range of opportunities in the business and administration departments of airport authorities and airline and travel companies. There are positions in such fields as sales and marketing, advertising, airline operations, engineering, finance, personnel, supplies and services, schedule planning, systems analysis, and organization and methods.

A bachelor's degree is needed for positions in these areas. Courses in accounting, business administration and management would provide good preparation.

Books

Careers in Airlines Operations, by Raymond Nathan, Walck, 1964. A comprehensive and practical survey of the airlines field; the advantages of each position; the education and qualifications needed.

Cleared for Takeoff: Behind the Scenes at an Airport, by Charles Coombs, William Morrow, 1969.

Airline Guide to Stewardess and Steward Careers, by Alexander C. Morton, Arco, 1975.

Your Future as an Airline Steward-Stewardess, by Lyman Randall, Rosen Press, 1973.

Your Future as a Pilot, by Kimball J. Scribner, Arco, 1971.

Anyone Can Fly, by Jules Bergman, Doubleday, 1977.

Useful words

Some useful words to know if you are thinking of working at an airport or in some other branch of aviation.

Aircraft hold area beneath the floor of an airliner cabin, where cargo and the passengers' luggage are carried.

Apron area of concrete where planes stop to load and unload passengers.

Boarding pass a piece of card, exchanged for the passenger's ticket, which every passenger has to have before he can go on a plane.

Cabin crew the stewards and stewardesses serving the passengers on a flight.

Carousel a revolving platform on which the passengers' luggage is delivered to them from the planes.

Concourse the big open area inside an airport building where passengers go to check in for flights.

Currency another word for money.

Duty-free shop a shop at airports where goods can be bought by passengers without paying tax on them.

Engine thrust the power produced by a jet engine, reckoned in pounds weight.

Flight deck also called the cockpit, where the flight crew sit to fly the plane.

▲ Refuelling a DC10.

Flight deck crew the pilots and flight engineer on the flight deck of an airliner.

Flight recorder an instrument like a tape recorder, enclosed in a steel box to withstand crashes, which tells how the plane has been flown.

Galley the kitchen in an airliner, where the meals and drinks are prepared by the cabin crew.

Interlining when passengers change planes at an airport.

Jumbo jet a Boeing 747 airliner, but often used to describe other big planes carrying hundreds of passengers.

Load sheet contains information relating to a plane's cargo, used for calculating the amount of fuel required.

Navigation the science used by pilots for finding their way around the sky.

Passport a booklet giving the name and carrying the photograph of its owner which has to be carried by every passenger who goes abroad.

Radar powerful radio beams which bounce off metal planes. These beams then show up on the screens used by air traffic controllers.

Radio beacon a radio wave given out by a station on the ground. This is picked up by a radio set in the planes and helps the pilots to work out their position in the sky.

Subsonic plane any plane which flies slower than the speed of sound (around 1,100 kmph).

Supersonic plane airliners flying faster than the speed of sound. The Concorde's top speed is 2,000 kmph.

Terminals airport buildings from which passengers board their planes.

Travel courier usually the employee of a travel agency who helps passengers at airports to find their planes.

Tug a specially-built, powerful truck which is used at airports to pull airliners away from the terminals.

X-ray a form of radiation which, when applied to passengers' luggage, shows up on a screen whether they have any metal objects such as guns inside.

Flying Know-How, by Robert N. Buck, Delacorte, 1975.

America's Flying Book, ed. by *Flying Magazine,* Scribner's 1972.

A and P General Handbook. An airframe and powerplant mechanics' handbook. Aviation Maintenance Publishers (Basin, Wyo.) 1978.

Airframe and Powerplant Mechanic Practical Tests, by Acme School of Aeronautics, Aviation (Milwaukee), 1976.

Airways to Airlines: 50 Year History of Commercial Aviation, Aviation, (Milwaukee), 1975.

Sky's the Limit: The History of the Airlines, by Charles J. Kelly, Arno, 1971.

Films

Rapid Transit in the Sky. Set of slides and cassette giving an overview of the air transport industry and its role in carrying passengers, mail, and freight. Available for borrowing from:

> Air Transport Association
> Attn.: Mr. W. G. Osmun
> AV Section
> 1709 New York Ave., N.W.
> Washington, D.C. 20006

The International Airline: Wings Around the World. Available for rental from:

> Vision Associates
> 665 Fifth Ave.
> New York, N.Y. 10022

The Airport: Gateway to the Skies. Available for rental from Vision Associates (see above).

How to Succeed Without Really Flying, 1971. An air traffic controller tells about his job. Available for rental from:

> Film Library
> AAC-44E
> Federal Aviation Administration
> P.O. Box 25082
> Oklahoma City, Okla. 73125

Acknowledgments

Key to the position of the illustrations: (T) top; (C) centre; (B) bottom; and combinations, for example: (TR) top right, or (CL) centre left.

Artists
Terry Allen Designs Ltd: 4-5, 16, 21
Hayward Art Group: 6-7, 17, 30-31 (B), 37
Roland Berry: 10-11
Ian Guy & Tom Stimpson/Ian Fleming & Associates: 12-13
John Shackell: 14, 18, 28, 38
Adrian Day/Ian Fleming & Associates: 22-23
Keith Harmer/Andrew Archer Associates: 30-31

Photographs
Spectrum: Jacket (front), 7 (TR), 32 (C)
Lufthansa German Airlines: jacket (back), 8 (B), 10, 15 (T), 24 (L), 35 (TL) (TR) (B)
Mike St Maur Sheil: 2, 9 (C), 21, 25 (TL) (B), 34 (L), 41 (C), 42 (C)
Shaun Skelly: 4, 5 (T) (BL) (BR)
ZEFA: 6 (T), 7 (C), 11 (R), 17, 19 (CL)
Courtesy of the Press Office, Frankfurt Airport: 6 (BL), 7 (TL), 28 (R), 37 (BL)
Daily Telegraph Colour Library: 6 (BR), 43 (BR)
Peter Shephard: 7 (B), 36 (T)
British Airways: 8 (T), 20 (B), 33 (T)
British Airports Authority: 9 (T), 34 (R), 36 (B), 37 (T)

Scandinavian Airlines System: 9 (B), 15 (B), 25 (TR), 43 (BL)
Singapore Airlines—a great way to fly: 11 (L)
Popperfoto: 14, 40-41 (T)
Smiths Industries Ltd: 16
Central Office of Information: 19 (T) (R)
Dept. of Transportation, Official Photograph, Dulles International Airport, Washington: 20 (T)
TWA: 24 (R)
British Caledonian Airways: 27 (C)
QANTAS: 27 (BL) (BR), 44, 45
Press Association: 28 (L)
British Aircraft Corporation: 29
Keystone Press Agency: 31 (T) (B), 33 (C) (B), 40 (C), 41 (BL)
London Ambulance Service: 31 (C)
Futura Publications: 32 (B)
KLM Dutch Airlines: 37 (BR)
Commissioner of Police, Metropolitan Branch: 41 (BR)
Transworld Feature Syndicate: 42-43 (T)
The Post Office: 43 (C)
H.M. Customs and Excise: 38-39, 39 (T) (B)

The Author and Publishers would like to acknowledge the help of British Caledonian Airways for the information on pages 22-23, and of Sperry Gyroscope, Bracknell, Berks, for permission to reproduce on pages 30-31 a print-out from their Sperry Sadas 5,000 flight recorder.

Index